Title: Measuring the ROI of being coached: Quantifying the Value of coaching for Personal Development.

Ryan V. Dawson

Introduction   3
Chapter 1: Embrace Your Inner Learner   5
Chapter 2: Finding Your Coaching Partner   10
Chapter 3: The Coaching Revolution   20
Chapter 4: Unleashing Your Leadership Potential 24
Chapter 5: Beyond the Comfort Zone   29
Chapter 6: Adapting to Change   39
Chapter 7: The ROI of Coaching   45
Conclusion   51
About the Author   57

Introduction

Meet Ryan V. Dawson, the author of "Measuring the ROI of Being Coached: Quantifying the Value of Coaching for Personal Development." But before we plunge into the realm of coaching, let's take some time to get to know the person behind the book.

Ryan's tale is one of sympathetic beginnings. Just like many of us, he started his job with ambitions and objectives but quickly found himself confronting problems and doubts. It was at these moments of self-doubt and thought that he discovered the wonderful power of coaching.

As a young professional, Ryan saw the transformative impact of coaching firsthand. With the help of a qualified coach, he was able to break through the hurdles holding him back, tap into his untapped potential, and set out on a road of personal growth and satisfaction. The trip was not without its ups and downs, but the impact was apparent.

Ryan's experiences with coaching created a desire inside him—a yearning to share this transformational energy with others. He became not just a believer in coaching but also a practitioner, committing himself to helping others unleash their inner potential and achieve their personal and professional goals.

In "Measuring the ROI of Being Coached," Ryan brings his personal and professional experience to life. Through his remarks, you'll sense his genuine excitement for coaching and his profound confidence in its capacity to alter lives. He smoothly integrates real-life experiences, practical ideas, and a personable attitude that makes the world of coaching accessible to anyone.

So, as we go on our trip via the pages of this book, remember that you're not only experiencing the transforming world of coaching; you're traveling with Ryan—a fellow traveler who knows the struggles and joys of personal growth. Together, we'll explore the mysteries of coaching, assess its impact, and learn how it may accelerate us toward personal transformation.

Welcome to the realm of coaching, guided by the wisdom and relatability of Ryan V. Dawson, where personal progress has no boundaries and every page carries the promise of unlocking your hidden potential.

Chapter 1: Embrace Your Inner Learner

Developing a coachable mindset

The Importance of Embracing Your Inner Learner

In an era marked by rapid technological breakthroughs, globalization, and altering economic landscapes, the concept of continual learning is no longer a luxury but a vital obligation. Here are some main reasons why engaging your inner learner is of critical importance:

1. Adaptation to Change: Change is the only constant thing in the modern world. Technology changes at a dizzying pace, businesses shift overnight, and global events reshape our lives. To flourish in such an atmosphere, one must possess the capacity to adapt quickly. Embracing your inner learner empowers you with the mental agility needed to manage these transitions effectively. It helps you lose the fear of the unknown and accept uncertainty as a chance for progress.

2. Personal Growth and Self-Discovery: Learning is not only about obtaining new knowledge or abilities; it's a transforming process that extends into every part of your life. It inspires introspection, challenges preconceived assumptions, and increases self-awareness. When you accept your inner learner, you go on a path of self-discovery. You uncover your talents, weaknesses, interests, and purpose. This personal growth path not only enriches your life but also strengthens your ability to contribute meaningfully to society.

3. Professional Success: In the sphere of work and profession, the benefits of lifelong learning cannot be stressed. Employers need workers who are not just skilled in their present responsibilities but also versatile and willing to gain new skills. By fostering your inner learner attitude, you make yourself

useful in the workplace. You become the employee who can pivot when required, overcome complicated situations, and lead teams with fresh ideas.

Cultivating the Inner Learner Mindset
Now that we've established the value of embracing your inner learner, let's discuss practical strategies to develop this mindset:

1. Stay Curious: Curiosity is the driving factor behind learning. It motivates you to explore new territory, ask questions, and seek deeper understanding. Cultivate your curiosity by actively searching out knowledge, engaging in thought-provoking conversations, and retaining a genuine interest in the world around you.

2. Embrace Failure as a Stepping Stone: Failure is not a sign of ineptitude but a stepping stone on the route to achievement. When you meet setbacks, regard them as important lessons. Analyze what went wrong, extract insights, and apply them to move yourself ahead.

3. Define clear learning goals: To get the most out of your learning journey, define clear and realistic goals. Define what you want to learn and why it matters to you. Goals give direction and motivation, ensuring that your learning efforts are purposeful and linked with your ambitions.

4. Make Learning a Daily Habit: Learning should not be restricted to formal schooling or intermittent spurts of interest. Make it a daily habit. Dedicate time in your calendar for

reading, discovering new talents, or taking online courses. The abundance of information in the digital era makes it simpler than ever to obtain knowledge.

5. Seek constructive feedback: Feedback is a vital tool for improvement. Seek input from mentors, peers, or via self-assessment. Constructive criticism helps you find areas for growth and polish your talents. It's a road to ongoing self-improvement.

6. Embrace Challenges: Don't shy away from challenges; embrace them. When you encounter obstacles and push your boundaries, you not only gain resilience but also learn new abilities and insights. Challenges excite your inner learner by providing possibilities for improvement.

7. Cultivate Patience: Learning is a journey that unfolds over time. Be patient with yourself. Avoid the temptation of expecting quick expertise. Instead, focus on steady growth and acknowledge that modest, incremental actions contribute to big knowledge and skill development.

8. Share Your Knowledge: Teaching others is a wonderful way to reinforce your own learning. When you share your expertise, you not only aid others on their learning journeys but also increase your own comprehension of the subject matter. This supports the concept that learning is a collaborative process that benefits everyone involved.

9. Stay open-minded: Maintain an open mind while encountering fresh ideas or opinions. Be willing to confront

your previous views and be open to change. An open-minded approach supports intellectual progress and prevents intellectual stagnation.

Embracing your inner learner is not a static achievement but a dynamic, continual commitment to growth and self-improvement. It's a purposeful decision to embrace curiosity, learn from setbacks, establish objectives, and actively seek chances to enhance your knowledge and abilities. In a society that encourages adaptation and lifelong learning, fostering your inner learner mentality is the key to prospering both personally and professionally. By taking that initial step on your journey of lifelong learning, you unlock the doors to a world of unlimited possibilities and pave the route for a satisfying, meaningful life. So, take the moment and let your inner learner blossom.

Chapter 2: Finding Your Coaching Partner

Navigating the Coach Selection Process

Coaching has become a vital aspect of personal and professional growth. Whether you're wanting to strengthen your leadership abilities, go through life transitions, or achieve particular goals, a coach may provide vital insight and support. However, not all coaches are made equal, and picking the correct one may be a key decision on your route to growth and success. Let's look at the process of hiring a coach, reviewing the major aspects, questions to ask, and measures to take to identify your ideal coaching partner.

Firstly, before delving into the selection process, it's necessary to grasp what coaching is all about. Let's immediately obtain an overview of coaching.

What is coaching? Coaching refers to the process of educating, coaching, or instructing a person or group on how to build abilities to boost their productivity or overcome a performance problem. The supervisor is termed a coach, while the learner is called the coach. Coaching approaches and models often entail careful observation, accountability, and feedback on development and performance.

Types of coaching.

There is no clear separation of coaches by form and kind of activity, although there are certain defined categories that are common:

1. Life coaching: A life coach is someone who counsels and motivates clients through personal or career issues. A life coach helps lead customers to accomplish their ultimate goals.

A life coach may help individuals in numerous aspects of their lives. But because each human being is different, so are their ambitions. Oftentimes, a life coach counsels individuals in personal and professional areas. This implies a job, personal growth, relationships, nutrition, divorce, sorrow, and even financial wellbeing.

2. Business coaching: Business coaching may benefit people in various sectors of employment. Whether it is executive coaching for senior managers, interview coaching for job seekers, or start-up company coaching for entrepreneurs, all have been shown to be hugely beneficial in completing an individual's objective.

3. Sport coaching: Sports coaching may be defined as the act of inspiring, directing, and preparing an individual in preparation for any sports pastime, career, or event.

4. Career coaches: helping individuals negotiate career choices, employment transfers, and skill development.

5. Specialized coaches: coaches with experience in particular areas like health and wellness, relationship coaching, or creativity.

The Benefits of Coaching: The benefits of coaching include:

- fine-tuning a skill
- increasing learning
- fixing challenges
- developing peak performance
- strategic planning
- producing change
- target identification, etc.

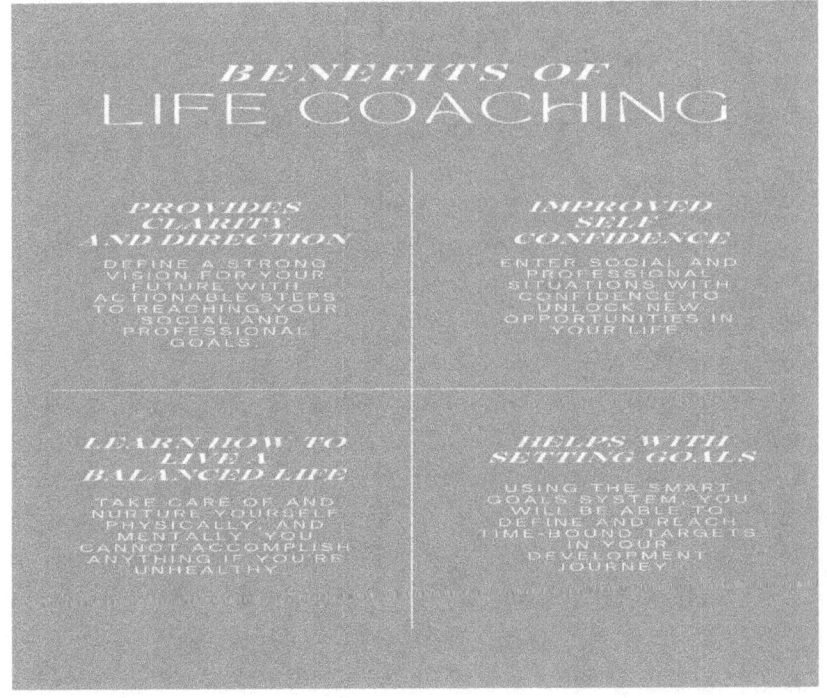

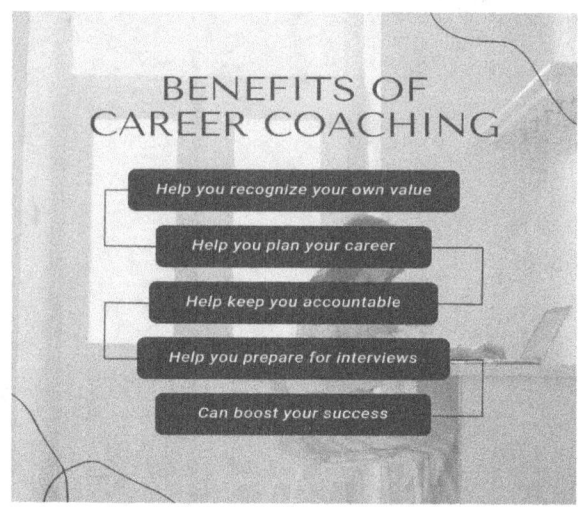

When to Seek a Coach: The beauty of coaching is that it may be obtained at many stages in life, according to your changing requirements and objectives. Here's a deeper look at when you can seek a coach:

1. Life changes: Life is marked by changes, both foreseen and unexpected. Whether you're beginning a new phase, like starting college, getting married, or retiring, or suffering an unexpected transition, such as a divorce or job loss, a coach may provide vital support. They can help you manage the uncertainties, create new objectives, and map a route forward.

2. Career Crossroads: Career selections typically demand considerable thinking. If you're at a professional crossroads—contemplating a job shift, pursuing a new role, or seeking career advancement—a career coach can advise you.

They aid with establishing your career objectives, formulating a strategic strategy, and increasing your professional abilities.

3. When Feeling Stuck: At times, life might feel stagnant, and you could feel imprisoned in a pattern that no longer suits you. A coach can help you understand the underlying causes of your stagnation, create fresh goals, and give you the responsibility and inspiration required to move ahead.

4. Improving Relationships: Struggling in personal relationships or encountering communication issues within your family or with a partner? Relationship coaches specialize in helping clients through these challenges. They give skills for successful communication, conflict resolution, and developing healthy connections.

5. Self-Discovery and Growth: Seeking a coach to stimulate personal growth and self-discovery is a wonderful proactive move. Whether you want to better your self-awareness, build confidence, or delve into your potential, a personal development coach may be your guide on this path.

6. Goal Achievement: If you have certain objectives in mind, such as weight reduction, fitness, or financial milestones, a coach might be crucial. They help you define SMART (specific, measurable, achievable, relevant, and time-bound) objectives, build action plans, and give you the support required to stay on track.

7. Health and Wellness: Wellness coaches focus on helping individuals make healthier lifestyle choices. Whether you want

to improve your nutrition, manage stress, or boost your general well-being, a wellness coach can give you direction and responsibility.

8. Time Management and Productivity: Struggling with time management and productivity? A coach can help you uncover time-wasting behaviors, design efficient routines, and prioritize work to enhance productivity.

9. Leadership Development: Leadership coaching is important for both aspiring and existing leaders. It assists in boosting leadership abilities, improving decision-making, and creating successful management techniques.

10. Overcoming Limiting Beliefs: If you're held back by limiting beliefs or negative thinking patterns that restrict your success, a coach can help you discover and fight these ideas. They aid you in changing your mentality to uncover your potential.

11. Dealing with Stress and Burnout: Coping with stress, anxiety, or burnout? A coach may provide stress management skills, resilience-building tactics, and tools to maintain a good work-life balance.

12. Accomplishing financial objectives: Managing funds properly and accomplishing financial objectives can be tough. Financial coaches give help on budgeting, saving, investing, and debt management to safeguard your financial future.

In summary, the answer to "When can I seek a coach?" is very flexible. Coaching is not restricted to any one phase or problem; it is flexible to your individual circumstances and goals. The key is identifying when you may benefit from the skills and support of a coach and being open to the transforming potential that coaching can bring. Whether you're seeking personal improvement, job progress, or navigating life's twists and turns, a coach may be your companion on the route to success and fulfillment.

Chapter 3: The Coaching Revolution

How Coaching Transforms Leadership

Coaching has a transforming influence on leadership by developing personal and professional growth, boosting self-awareness, and strengthening leadership abilities. Here's how coaching can alter leadership:

1. Discovering Your True Self: Imagine coaching as a mirror that helps leaders see themselves more clearly. It unveils your talents, limitations, and values, almost like unearthing buried

treasure within. This heightened self-awareness becomes the compass directing your leadership path.

2. Speaking the vocabulary of connection: coaching offers leaders the vocabulary of empathy and understanding. Picture it as a translator that lets you connect with your team on a deeper level. You learn to talk not just with words but also with true compassion and feeling.

3. Navigating Life's Rapids: Just like a river guide helps you manage difficult waters, coaching empowers leaders to steer through the turbulent currents of change. It's like having a reliable paddle in the form of resilience and adaptation, helping you to weather any storm.

4. Solving Puzzles with Clarity: Leadership frequently seems like solving complicated puzzles. Coaches bring clarity, serving as your puzzle-solving partner. They help you piece together information, analyze possibilities, and make decisions confidently.

5. The Building Blocks of Trust: Coaching improves the basis of trust within your team. It's like constructing a trust bridge between you and your colleagues. This bridge helps you to cross challenging talks and disagreements with greater comfort and understanding.

6. Writing Your Leadership Story: Think of coaching as helping you develop your leadership story. It allows you to establish objectives, develop your story, and take charge of your path.

Your coach becomes the editor, helping you improve and shape your narrative.

7. The Flexible Leadership Dance: Just as a dancer adapts to new rhythms and styles, coaching teaches leaders the skill of flexibility. You become a versatile dancer, seamlessly moving between leadership styles to match the particular demands of your team and difficulties.

8. Resilience in the Face of Adversity: Coaching is like an inner resilience coach. It helps you bounce back from setbacks and hardships. Think of it as having a mental gym that develops your capacity to handle hardship head-on.

9. Bridging the Gap with Communication: Leaders often experience communication gaps. Coaching functions as the bridge builder, helping you transcend these gaps with efficient communication. You become a good communicator who can explain ideas clearly and motivate your team.

10. Guiding the Ship Through Storms: Imagine coaching as your leadership lighthouse, guiding your ship through the hardest storms. It illuminates your route and helps you stay on track, even when the waves grow choppy.

11. Painting Your Leadership Canvas: Coaching pushes leaders to become painters of invention and creativity. It's like handing you a paintbrush to create a masterpiece of creative ideas and answers.

12. Unlocking the Potential of Others: Just as a coach helps you reach your full potential, coaching equips leaders to unlock the hidden potential of their team members. You become a coach within your team, nurturing growth and excellence.

13. Cultivating Confidence and Empathy: Coaching boosts your confidence, making you a more confident leader. Simultaneously, it cultivates empathy, allowing you to truly understand the perspectives and feelings of others.

14. Measuring Success on Your Journey: Coaching is like setting milestones on your leadership journey. As you achieve these goals, it's akin to reaching scenic viewpoints along the way. These milestones reinforce your belief in the transformative power of coaching.

In essence, coaching is your trusted companion on the leadership adventure, helping you navigate, connect, adapt, and thrive. It empowers you to be the best leader you can be, both for yourself and for your team.

Chapter 4: Unleashing Your Leadership Potential

Strategies for growth and development

Personal growth and development are lifetime journeys that involve purposeful effort and tactics to attain genuine improvement. Whether you're wanting to enhance your talents, increase your knowledge, or become a better version of yourself, here are some excellent techniques to promote your growth and development:

1. Set Clear Goals with Heart: Start by defining goals that actually matter to you. What do you want to achieve, and why? When your objectives are connected with your passions and beliefs, you'll discover the desire to pursue them fiercely.

2. Learning as a Lifelong Adventure: Treat learning as an enjoyable adventure rather than a work. Dive into books, courses, and experiences that excite your curiosity. Remember, the journey of learning is as essential as the destination.

3. Self-Reflection: Your Personal Compass Regularly pause to reflect on your life's path. What have you gained from your experiences? How can you utilize these insights to grow

further? Self-reflection is like your personal compass, directing you on your way.

4. Embrace Mentorship and Be a Mentor: Seek mentors who inspire you and mentors whom you can influence. This two-way link fosters progress. Learn from people with more experience, and share your expertise with those who need help.

5. The Power of Authentic Connections: Networking is more than just collecting business cards. Cultivate honest interactions with others who share your interests and beliefs. These relationships will help your progress and give you vital insights.

6. Time Management as a Self-Care Act: Efficient time management is a sort of self-care. It guarantees that you dedicate time not only for work but also for things that foster your personal growth, such as hobbies, exercise, and leisure.

7. Health is wealth for progress: A healthy body and mind are the cornerstones of personal progress. Prioritize your physical and emotional well-being via frequent exercise, appropriate eating, and mindfulness activities.

8. Dare to Step Out of Your Comfort Zone: Growth frequently happens beyond your comfort zone. Challenge yourself with new experiences, whether it's learning a new skill, traveling to foreign areas, or taking on new responsibilities.

9. Input is a Gift: Seek input from reputable sources. It's a gift that helps you progress. Remember that feedback is not a reflection on your value but a chance for progress.

10. Capture Insights Through Journaling: Keeping a diary is like gathering fireflies of insight. Write down your thoughts, experiences, and ideas. It's a fantastic tool for self-discovery and charting your progress.

11. Mindfulness and Meditation: Nurture Your Inner Garden Mindfulness and meditation are like caring for the garden of your inner self. They help you increase self-awareness, alleviate stress, and develop emotional intelligence.

12. Paint Your Success Story: Imagine your own growth path as a painting. You wield the paintbrush. Every decision and action adds color to your masterpiece. Paint the tale you wish to tell.

13. Unlock Your Inner Resilience: Life will bring hurdles your way. Your resilience is your protection. It's not about avoiding misfortune but about rebounding stronger each time.

14. Building Bridges with Effective Communication: Communication is the bridge that links you with others. Effective communication increases understanding and teamwork. Hone your listening and speaking abilities.

15. A Symphony of Gratitude: Gratitude is the song that fills your life with delight. Create a daily or weekly thankfulness practice. It might be as basic as scribbling down things you're grateful for.

16. Providing Feedback as a Gift: Just as you want feedback, provide it to others as a gift. Constructive feedback helps not

just the recipient but also strengthens your communication and leadership abilities.

17. Give Back and Shine Together: Volunteer your time or support causes you're passionate about. Giving back to your community or a cause provides a meaningful layer to your own growth path.

18. Your Goals, Your Rhythm: Regularly evaluate and change your goals to suit your developing priorities. Life is a dynamic dance, and your objectives should flow with your beat.

19. Rejoice the Small Wins: Don't wait for great victories to rejoice. Acknowledge and applaud even the slightest steps forward. These festivities drive your motivation.

20. Self-Talk Shapes Your reality: Be attentive to your self-talk. Replace self-doubt with positive affirmations. These affirmations modify your mentality and enhance your self-confidence.

21. Craft Your Personal Development Plan: Develop an organized plan that includes your goals, methods, and dates. Think of it as a treasure map pointing you to personal growth riches.

Remember, personal growth and development are not linear paths. There will be ups and downs, twists and turns. Embrace the journey, celebrate the minor successes, and stay true to your own path of progress. Your path is a continuous, magnificent tale ready to be told, one chapter at a time.

Chapter 5: Beyond the Comfort Zone

Integrating coaching into personal and professional growth

In the pursuit of personal and professional progress, there is an intrinsic desire to explore unfamiliar territory, break the bonds of familiarity, and travel into the unknown. Coaching, at its essence, is a collaborative journey of self-discovery and progress. It encourages individuals to tap into their latent potential, overcome problems, and create ambitious objectives. The coaching relationship, whether in a personal or professional environment, relies on a foundation of trust, honest discussion, and a commitment to growth. It is this very devotion that pulls people beyond their comfort zones.

Imagine coaching as a trusted companion, going beside you through the maze of personal and professional growth. It's like having a smart buddy who nudges you out of your comfort zone and into the realm of possibilities. In this article, we'll discuss how incorporating coaching into both the personal and professional sides of life drives you into unknown territory, where actual transformation occurs.

Coaching isn't simply a method; it's an experience. Picture it as a catalyst for transformation, kindling the fire within you to travel beyond your comfort zone.

The Comfort Zone's Trap
The comfort zone, as the name indicates, is a psychological region where individuals feel comfortable, secure, and unchallenged. It's a zone of familiarity where routines are predictable and dangers are reduced. Your comfort zone is that comfortable area where everything feels familiar, secure, and predictable. But here's the twist: While comfort zones serve as a haven during times of stress, they hold you back from growing. They also indicate stagnation—a zone where personal and professional progress grinds to a standstill.

Integrating coaching is like pushing open the door to a world beyond your comfort zone. It's about asking yourself tough questions, testing your self-imposed constraints, and daring to dream big. It's removing the idea that your comfort zone is a fortress when, in reality, it's a gilded prison.

Personal Growth: The Inner Journey

Discovering Your True Self: Coaching guides you on a path of self-discovery. It invites you to peel back the layers, expose your genuine self, and confront your innermost desires. As you delve deeper, you find that your comfort zone covers your genuine objectives.

Setting Audacious Goals: Coaching pushes you to break away from self-imposed restrictions. Coaches help you dream bigger and develop objectives that stretch your limitations. They lead you step-by-step, pushing you beyond your comfort zone. With each step, you learn that your comfort zone is a self-imposed barrier, not a sanctuary.

Embracing Vulnerability: Leaving your comfort zone is embracing vulnerability. It means entering into the unknown, where achievement and failure coexist. Coaching gives you the resilience to flourish amid unpredictability. Setbacks become stepping stones, and vulnerability evolves into a source of strength.

Professional Growth: Elevating Your Career

Becoming a Leader: In the working environment, coaching is your compass for leadership growth. Leaders regularly tread unfamiliar seas, make challenging decisions, and steer teams through uncertainty. Coaches arm you with the skills and mentality to flourish in challenging circumstances.

Unlocking Creativity: Workplaces thrive on innovation and innovative thought, frequently confined within your comfort zone. Coaching motivates you to think differently, to accept measured risks, and to celebrate ideas. It teaches you that failure is a stepping stone to achievement.

Mastering Conflict and Team Dynamics: Effective communication, conflict resolution, and team dynamics are crucial at work. Yet, confronting these difficulties may be uncomfortable. Coaches provide you with the tools to negotiate these situations with expertise and grace.

Integration: A Symphony of Growth
The beauty of incorporating coaching into personal and professional growth rests in its comprehensive character. It understands that these two realities are interrelated, with each impacting the other.

Cross-Pollination of Insights
Insights from personal growth frequently transcend into your work life. For example, heightened self-awareness and resilience acquired personally strengthen your leadership qualities. The courage to overcome personal anxieties empowers you to meet working obstacles with greater confidence.

Conversely, talents mastered professionally, such as excellent communication or dispute resolution, frequently help your personal connections. Strategies used to handle job issues may be adapted to interpersonal interactions, leading to better and more meaningful relationships.

The Confidence Cascade

Stepping outside your comfort zone in any domain builds your confidence. The bravery to take measured risks crosses over into your professional objectives. You become more inclined to seek ambitious objectives and accept leadership jobs.

In exchange, the professional successes won by addressing pain generate self-assurance that translates into personal progress. You become more robust, adaptive, and receptive to personal difficulties.

Alignment in Values and Purpose
As you go further into your personal growth path, you typically realize your underlying values and life purpose. These insights shape your decisions, including your job path and professional objectives. You want alignment between your personal ideals and those supported in your work life.

Coaching is your guiding star, illuminating your path and calling you to leave your comfort zone and explore the unfamiliar. It's a mirror reflecting your genuine self, a catalyst for creativity, and a bridge connecting personal and professional progress.

Embracing transformation via coaching isn't a solo process. It's a symphony of growth echoing throughout all dimensions of your existence. It urges you to dance on the brink of discomfort, where deep transformation and unlimited possibilities await. As you begin on this unknown route, you learn that the secret to your progress resides in accepting the difficulty of leaving your comfort zone.

Lifelong learning and leadership excellence

Imagine a leader standing at the helm of a ship, navigating the unpredictable waters of change. The leader's dilemma is clear: to remain stationary is to fall behind. In an era of fast technological breakthroughs, shifting demographics, and ever-changing market dynamics, leaders must adapt or risk becoming outdated. Leadership isn't only about giving commands or making choices; it's about motivating and directing others toward a common objective. It's a difficult, varied position that demands ongoing growth and development. This is when lifelong learning enters the stage.

Lifelong learning is the cornerstone of leadership excellence because it helps leaders adapt to change effectively. It's an awareness that the playbook of yesterday might not work tomorrow. Leaders who commit to learning recognize that keeping flexible and open-minded is crucial to navigating the rough seas of change.

Take the example of a seasoned CEO. In an ever-evolving industry, they know that to remain at the helm successfully, they must regularly educate themselves about emerging technology, market trends, and creative management practices. This flexibility is not only relatable but vital in today's fast-paced society.

Empathy and communication
Leadership is also about knowing and engaging with people. Lifelong learning helps leaders acquire critical soft skills, such

as empathy and effective communication. These qualities help leaders to relate to their team members, understand their issues, and establish a culture of trust and collaboration.

Think about a middle manager at a global firm. They recognize that leadership isn't only about hitting objectives; it's about creating connections with people from varied backgrounds. Lifelong learning helps people strengthen their multicultural communication skills, creating a more inclusive work atmosphere.

Innovation and problem-solving

Innovation is the lifeblood of any successful firm. Leaders who commit to lifelong learning are more likely to develop a culture of creativity within their teams. They're open to new ideas, willing to experiment, and fearful of failure.

Consider an entrepreneur creating a startup. They recognize that to flourish in a competitive market, they must continually seek new solutions, gain new skills, and change their plans. Lifelong learning becomes not only a choice but a survival strategy.

Ethical Leadership

Leadership greatness isn't only about attaining goals; it's about doing so ethically and responsibly. Lifelong learning helps leaders stay knowledgeable about ethical behaviors, societal duties, and the ramifications of their actions.

Imagine a government person responsible for policies. They recognize that their actions touch the lives of numerous people. Lifelong learning ensures they stay well-versed in shifting societal requirements and ethical issues, ensuring they lead with integrity.

Lifelong Learning in Practice
Reading as a Habit
A practical strategy to embrace lifelong learning is to make reading a habit. Leaders typically mention reading as a main source of information and inspiration. Reading broadly, from books on leadership and management to industry-specific periodicals, broadens horizons and keeps leaders informed.

Mentorship and networking
Another applicable route for continual learning is mentorship and networking. Leaders might seek assistance and mentorship from more experienced colleagues or industry experts. Through networking, they receive ideas from various viewpoints and remain current on developing trends.

Online courses and workshops
In today's digital world, online courses and seminars offer accessible and flexible learning options. Leaders may make use of platforms like Coursera, edX, or LinkedIn Learning to gain new skills and information relevant to their jobs.

Learning from failure
Failure is a potent teacher. Leaders should embrace failures as useful learning opportunities. Analyzing what went wrong and how to improve is an important element of lifelong learning. It's through failures that leaders typically uncover their greatest qualities.

The Relatability Factor

The beauty of the relationship between lifelong learning and leadership excellence is its relatability. It's a connection that doesn't apply simply to business CEOs or political leaders. It applies to everyone, from parents attempting to lead and nurture their families to community leaders fighting for constructive change.

Parenting as leadership

Parenting, for instance, is a sort of leadership. Lifelong learning in parenting requires adjusting to the changing needs of children, recognizing the complexities of their growth, and always exploring ways to be a better caregiver and role model.

Community Leadership

Community leaders, too, benefit from lifelong learning. Whether it's recognizing growing community needs, practicing effective communication to motivate volunteers, or being knowledgeable about local legislation, constant learning is crucial.

Educators and Lifelong Learning

Even educators, who play a vital role in creating future leaders, benefit from lifelong learning. Staying informed on pedagogical innovations, educational technology, and increasing student requirements is crucial for their efficacy.

Lifelong Learning as a Universal Journey

In the fabric of life, leadership isn't restricted to business boardrooms or government positions. It's a global notion, ingrained into the fabric of our daily lives. Lifelong learning, the ongoing pursuit of knowledge and improvement, is the thread that unites leadership and greatness for everyone.

As we negotiate the ever-changing landscapes of our personal and professional positions, we must remember that leadership isn't a set destination. It's a dynamic journey, a commitment to constant learning and growth—a path that transforms us into leaders, not only by title but by action and influence.

Chapter 6: Adapting to Change

Thriving in a Dynamic Business Landscape

Picture your favorite bakery. You've been visiting there for years, and you've come to enjoy their famous chocolate chip cookies. But one day, you go in, and you find a new offering—matcha green tea biscuits. Change may be as easy as that, or it can be as difficult as a total redesign of how a firm functions. Change is the only constant in the world of business. Whether you're a seasoned entrepreneur, a small business owner, or someone just starting out, adjusting to change is vital for surviving in today's changing business market. In this post, we'll break down the notion of adapting to change into accessible and easy words, providing you with practical insights to flourish in the ever-evolving corporate environment.

The Nature of Change

Change in the corporate sector may take various shapes. It may be a rapid shift in client preferences, a new rival joining the market, technological developments, or even external causes like economic downturns or world disasters (sound familiar, like a specific pandemic?). The point is that change is not something we can escape, but something we must accept and handle.

The Resistance to Change

Before we go into how to adapt, let's accept that humans, especially company owners and staff, typically resist change. It's normal to feel comfortable with what we know, and change might interrupt that comfort. However, it's vital to remember that rejecting change can limit development and creativity.

Why should we adapt to change?

Before we investigate how to adapt, let's grasp why it's so important:

1. Stay competitive.
In a changing corporate market, being competitive is a daily fight. Your rivals are undoubtedly adapting to change, and if you don't, you risk slipping behind.

2. Meet customer expectations.
Customers' requirements and tastes vary over time. Adapting to these changes ensures you continue to exceed their expectations and keep their loyalty.

3. Innovate and grow.

Change frequently opens doors to creativity. Businesses that accept change might uncover new goods, services, or processes that fuel development and expansion.

4. Attract and retain talent.

Today's workforce values versatility. Businesses that embrace change tend to recruit and keep top personnel who are enthused about being part of a dynamic workplace.

5. Mitigate risks.

Change can also bring hazards, but adaptive firms are better suited to detect and handle these risks efficiently.

6. Embrace Opportunities

Change frequently gives new chances. Being open to change means you may grasp these possibilities and use them to expand your business.

7. Survive and thrive

In hard times, firms that adapt are more likely to survive and even grow. Flexibility and adaptation may be a lifeline amid economic downturns.

The Barriers to Change

Change may be like climbing a mountain—daunting and fraught with hurdles. There are common challenges that firms experience while trying to adapt:

Fear of the Unknown

Change typically generates uncertainty, and the dread of the unknown may inhibit decision-making. People naturally oppose what they don't comprehend.

Resistance to Change

People are creatures of habit, and change upsets patterns. Employees and executives alike may oppose change owing to the discomfort it creates.

Lack of resources

Sometimes, adjusting involves resources like time, money, or technology that a firm may not have readily accessible.

Poor Communication

Effective communication is vital during times of transition. Without effective communication, employees may feel left in the dark, leading to uncertainty and resistance.

How to Adapt to Change

Now that we understand why it's necessary to adapt, let's explore some practical strategies to achieve it:

1. Embrace a growth mindset.

A growth mentality is the cornerstone of adaptability. It's about thinking that you can gain new talents and abilities through work and study. In both work and life, this perspective helps you perceive problems as chances for progress.

2. Stay informed.

Knowledge is power. Keep a tight watch on your industry, rivals, and market developments. Subscribe to industry magazines, attend webinars, and network with colleagues. The more you know, the more you can predict and adapt to change.

3. Be flexible.
Flexibility is a crucial attribute of successful enterprises. Your company model may need alterations from time to time. If a given product or service isn't functioning as intended, be open to pivoting or trying something new.

4. Involve Your Team
Your staff is your biggest asset. Encourage open communication and collaboration among your team. They may provide significant insights and ideas for adjusting to change efficiently.

5. Learn continuously.
In a changing corporate context, ongoing learning is vital. The same applies to personal growth; never stop learning, whether it's developing new skills, increasing information, or exploring new hobbies.

6. Embrace technology.
Technology is frequently a driving force behind change. Embrace technology as a tool to better your business operations, whether it's automating processes, extending your web presence, or using data analytics to make educated decisions.

7. Seek feedback.

Feedback is a key tool for adaptation. In business, input from consumers and workers can drive improvements. In personal interactions, requesting and providing criticism develops development and understanding.

8. Stay resilient.
Resilience is the capacity to bounce back from adversity. It's a vital characteristic in both work and life. Resilience permits you to adapt in the face of hardship and emerge stronger.

Chapter 7: The ROI of Coaching

Measuring the Value of Personal Transformation

How do we assess the worth of personal transformation? It's a question that prompts us to study the return on investment (ROI) of coaching, a potent motivator for transformation. In this detailed investigation, we will explore the subtleties of quantifying the profound worth of human development and the quantifiable ROI of coaching.

Personal development is a significant journey of self-discovery, growth, and change. It's the process of changing into a better version of oneself—physically, cognitively, emotionally, and spiritually. It includes different facets of life, from professions and relationships to health and thinking. One of the intrinsic obstacles to human development is the difficulty of assessing its worth. Unlike material possessions or financial benefits, personal growth frequently develops gradually, and its impacts may not be immediately obvious. This intricacy brings us to the essential function of coaching in assessing this value.

The value of personal transformation
Defining value in human change extends much beyond surface measures. It incorporates intangible characteristics like greater well-being, self-confidence, enhanced relationships, and a stronger sense of purpose. These aspects increase the quality of life and are essentially valued. However, personal transformation also offers practical advantages. For instance, greater communication abilities may lead to job progress, while enhanced emotional intelligence can build stronger relationships. These results are quantifiable and add to the ROI of coaching.

Quantifying the ROI of coaching

Return on investment (ROI) is a financial statistic used to analyze the profitability of an investment. In the context of coaching, it's about analyzing the returns (benefits) relative to the investment (time and resources). Calculating ROI bridges the gap between personal transformation's intangible worth and quantitative consequences. To evaluate the ROI of coaching, one must define and assess particular, quantifiable outcomes. These might be professional improvements, income rises, greater job satisfaction, lower stress levels, or healthier lifestyle choices. Each outcome is a component of the broader puzzle. In addition to quantifiable achievements, the ROI of coaching incorporates intangible rewards. These are frequently the most powerful and life-changing components of personal development, such as enhanced self-awareness, improved relationships, and a heightened sense of purpose. While they are tough to assess numerically, their influence is apparent.

ROI of coaching in professional contexts: Enhanced Leadership Skills: Leadership development is a typical area where coaching is applied. The ROI of coaching for leaders includes enhanced decision-making, stronger team cooperation, and the capacity to negotiate difficult situations efficiently. These benefits translate into enhanced team productivity and, frequently, revenue growth.

Career progress: For those pursuing career progress, coaching can be a strategic investment. It prepares individuals with the skills, confidence, and tactics needed to thrive in their positions and stand out in competitive circumstances. The ROI here is demonstrated in promotions, compensation rises, and greater responsibilities.

Entrepreneurship and Business Growth: Entrepreneurs and business owners can receive a large ROI from coaching. They get insights into company strategy, effective management, and creative techniques. The upshot is frequently greater profitability, corporate expansion, and a better market presence.

ROI of Coaching in Personal Growth

Improved Well-Being: Personal growth coaching focuses on holistic well-being. Clients find gains in mental health, less stress, better self-esteem, and higher life happiness. The ROI in this context is a life filled with joy, fulfillment, and resilience.

Health and Fitness: Coaching may also promote transformations in health and fitness. Individuals who invest in coaching may achieve weight loss, an improved diet, and greater physical activity. The ROI here is not just a healthier body but also a longer and more active life.

Enhanced Relationships: Coaching typically enhances relationships, both personal and professional. Clients learn effective communication, conflict resolution, and empathy. The ROI emerges in deeper connections, fewer disputes, and more meaningful relationships.

Measuring ROI: Tools and Approaches

Self-Assessment and Goal Tracking: One technique to estimate ROI is through self-assessment and goal tracking. Clients set precise targets at the outset of their coaching relationship and track their progress toward these goals. This strategy delivers a tangible sense of success.

Surveys and Feedback: Collecting feedback from clients and their coworkers can give insights into the impact of coaching. Surveys might monitor changes in leadership abilities, team dynamics, or work satisfaction. Positive comments and greater involvement generally indicate a successful ROI.

Comparative Analysis: Comparative analysis entails comparing the before-and-after events. For instance, a leader's performance measures, such as project success rates or team productivity, may be compared before and after coaching. This technique quantifies the improvements.

Challenges and Limitations in Measuring ROI Subjectivity and Individual Differences: Measuring the ROI of coaching can be tricky owing to the subjectivity of human growth. Each individual's experience is unique, making it impossible to use conventional measurements. Moreover, human growth is impacted by various elements outside of coaching.

Long-Term vs. Short-Term Outcomes: ROI evaluation frequently focuses on short-term results, such as quick career progression or better work satisfaction. However, the significant benefit of human development may continue to emerge over the long term, making it hard to capture entirely.

External variables: External variables, such as market conditions or personal circumstances, might alter the outcomes ascribed to coaching. Separating the influence of coaching from these external circumstances may be hard.

Maximizing ROI and sustaining transformation
Setting Clear Goals: To optimize ROI, clients and coaches must create clear, explicit goals at the outset of the coaching

partnership. These goals serve as milestones for monitoring development and analyzing the impact of coaching.

Continuous Learning and Application: To continue the advantages of coaching and optimize ROI, individuals must apply what they've learned continuously. This entails constant learning, practice, and self-reflection.

Feedback and Evaluation: Regular feedback and evaluation are vital. Clients should offer feedback to their coaches, allowing for improvements in coaching tactics. Additionally, periodic reviews help monitor progress toward goals.

While the ROI of coaching gives a quantitative viewpoint, the inestimable worth of personal development rests in its deep influence on our lives. It's the intangible sense of fulfillment, the better well-being, the deeper relationships, and the unchanging sense of purpose that actually define its worth. Personal development, fuelled by coaching, transcends basic numbers; it's a precious journey toward becoming the best version of oneself.

Conclusion

Let's put this research to a close by viewing these five amazing stories of coaching triumphs:

1. From Stagnation to Entrepreneurial Success
Sarah had long cherished a desire to become an entrepreneur, but for years, she felt confined in her unfulfilling corporate position. The dread of failure held her back, and she lacked the courage and direction to make her ambition a reality. That's when she decided to seek the counsel of a professional coach.

Through a series of coaching sessions, Sarah began to articulate her goals and desires. Her coach helped her discover her particular abilities and talents, and they worked together to construct a sound business strategy that resonated with her goal. But coaching wasn't only about establishing objectives; it was also about confronting the deep-seated fear of failure that had been holding her back.

With the continuing support and encouragement from her coach, Sarah took the plunge and launched her own internet marketing agency. It wasn't always simple, but she had the tools and mentality to tackle problems that emerged along the way. Over time, her firm began to develop, gaining clients who respected her skills and devotion.

Today, Sarah not only enjoys the financial advantages of her business endeavor but also finds tremendous happiness in pursuing her passion. Her journey from stagnation to entrepreneurial success is a tribute to the transforming power of coaching, which not only armed her with practical abilities but also instilled in her the courage to achieve her aspirations.

2. Overcoming Career Obstacles

John had always been a committed IT manager, but his career had reached a tough spot. He was suffering from team dynamics, and his communication skills required development. Projects were slipping behind schedule, and he was at risk of losing his job. That's when he decided to seek coaching.

His coach worked closely with John to discover the unique issues he was having. They concentrated on developing his leadership abilities, boosting his interactions with team members, and applying successful project management practices. John also learned useful tactics for dispute resolution and team building, abilities that were crucial for his work.

With persistence and the advice of his coach, John progressively improved his leadership style and team dynamics. His initiatives began to flow smoothly, and his team members felt more motivated and involved. His efforts didn't go unnoticed by upper management.

Not only did John maintain his work, but he also obtained a well-deserved promotion. Today, he is a recognized leader inside his firm, admired for his ability to overcome professional challenges and motivate his team to thrive. His tale is a brilliant example of how coaching can turn a career around, giving individuals the tools and insights needed to overcome professional problems.

3. Finding Purpose After Retirement

Maria had always been a passionate teacher, but after retiring, she found herself at a loss. The sense of purpose that came with her profession was abruptly lacking, and she sought to fill the hole. Unsure of what to do with her newfound free time, she decided to try coaching.

Through counseling, Maria went on a path of self-discovery. Her coach helped her through a process of reflection, helping her uncover her passions and interests beyond her teaching position. It became evident that teaching had been a tremendous source of joy for her, and she wanted to continue making a difference.

With her coach's backing, Maria decided to explore a new teaching position. She acquired a teaching credential and began working with poor youngsters in her town. The sense of purpose and joy she felt in educating these youngsters was tremendous. It was a chance for her to give back and continue doing what she loved most.

Maria's retirement years took on a new significance as she committed herself to having a positive effect on the lives of others. Her tale serves as a strong reminder that it's never too late to discover meaning and make a difference, even in the most unexpected ways.

4. Triumph over personal challenges

Dave, a young musician with enormous skill, has been battling with terrible anxiety and self-doubt for years. These personal problems were keeping him from following his passion for music and sharing his creativity with the world. Frustrated and on the verge of giving up, he turned to coaching for aid.

Dave's coach provided him with a secure environment to address his worries and self-limiting beliefs. They worked together on techniques to control his anxiety, increase his self-confidence, and create reasonable goals for his music career. Dave also learned ways to manage performance anxiety, a key challenge for him as a musician.

With constant encouragement from his coach, Dave began to take modest steps toward his objective. He started playing at local places and releasing his songs online. As he acquired experience and favorable feedback, his confidence continued to rise.

Dave's trip was not without its hurdles, but he persevered. He launched his debut album, which gained appreciation from both audiences and music journalists. Today, he inspires others not just with his music but also with his narrative of triumph over personal hardships. His story reveals the transforming potential of coaching in helping individuals overcome inner difficulties and accomplish their creative objectives.

5. A Journey from Burnout to Well-Being

Emma was a high-achieving professional who had climbed the corporate ladder with perseverance and commitment. However, her dogged pursuit of achievement had taken a toll on her health and well-being. She was feeling burnout, high stress levels, and a sense of emptiness in her life.

Recognizing the need for change, Emma sought the aid of a coach. In their counseling sessions, Emma and her coach looked into the fundamental causes of her burnout. They examined her beliefs, priorities, and the necessity of work-life balance. It was a journey of serious self-reflection and rediscovery.

Through counseling, Emma learned mindfulness techniques to manage stress and recover a sense of balance in her life. She learned to set boundaries and prioritize self-care, both at work and in her personal life. As a consequence, her physical and mental health improved, and she began to enjoy a renewed sense of purpose and satisfaction.

Emma's metamorphosis was amazing. She continued to flourish in her job, but this time she did it with greater attention to her well-being. Her experience serves as a reminder that gaining success doesn't have to come at the price of one's health and happiness. Emma's path from burnout to well-being is a witness to the transforming power of coaching on all parts of life, including physical and emotional well-being, and the significance of finding balance in the pursuit of success.

About the Author

Ryan V. Dawson is a prominent expert in the field of coaching. Drawing on a rich experience in psychology and leadership, Dawson's insights are not only academically sophisticated but also remarkably practical. He has a remarkable gift for making the complex principles of coaching accessible to a wide audience.

As an engaging speaker and renowned coach, Dawson has impacted the lives of many individuals, helping them uncover their hidden potential. His passion for personal development and building compassionate connections pours through in his work, making it relevant and meaningful.

Dawson's commitment to the advancement of humanity through personal development is clear in "Measuring the ROI of being coached." Through this book, he shares his enormous experience, enabling readers to traverse the nuances of feeling worthless, foster strong will, and achieve success through embracing your inner learner at its foundation. Ryan V. Dawson is a luminary in the area of personal development and his work continues to inspire and encourage individuals on the journey to becoming coachable masters.

www.ingramcontent.com/pod-product-compliance
Lightning Source LLC
Chambersburg PA
CBHW062300290526
45794CB00006B/2628